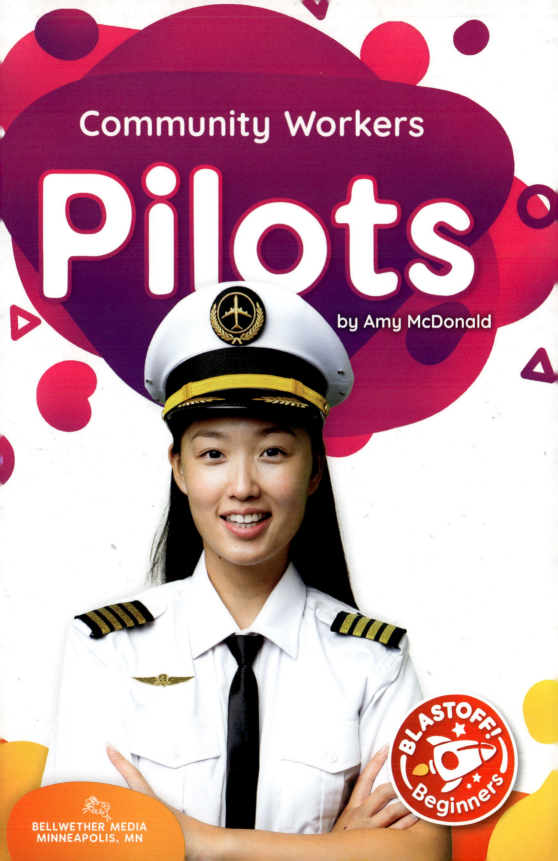

Blastoff! Beginners are developed by literacy experts and educators to meet the needs of early readers. These engaging informational texts support young children as they begin reading about their world. Through simple language and high frequency words paired with crisp, colorful photos, Blastoff! Beginners launch young readers into the universe of independent reading.

Sight Words in This Book

a	from	long	to
and	get	people	use
are	go	sit	way
away	have	the	we
can	in	they	
find	it	time	

This edition first published in 2025 by Bellwether Media, Inc.

No part of this publication may be reproduced in whole or in part without written permission of the publisher. For information regarding permission, write to Bellwether Media, Inc., Attention: Permissions Department, 6012 Blue Circle Drive, Minnetonka, MN 55343.

Library of Congress Cataloging-in-Publication Data

LC record for Pilots available at: https://lccn.loc.gov/2024038078

Text copyright © 2025 by Bellwether Media, Inc. BLASTOFF! BEGINNERS and associated logos are trademarks and/or registered trademarks of Bellwether Media, Inc.

Editor: Betsy Rathburn   Designer: Laura Sowers

Printed in the United States of America, North Mankato, MN.

Table of Contents

On the Job	4
What Are They?	6
What Do They Do?	10
Why Do We Need Them?	20
Pilot Facts	22
Glossary	23
To Learn More	24
Index	24

On the Job

The pilots are ready. Time to fly!

What Are They?

Pilots fly airplanes or **helicopters**. They sit in **cockpits**.

helicopter

cockpit

They take
people places.
They can fly
a long way.

What Do They Do?

Pilots wear **uniforms**. They have hats and ties.

They check the **aircraft**. They get it ready to fly.

They take off!
They use controls
to steer.

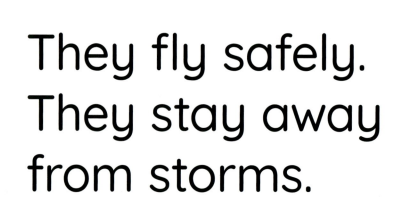

They fly safely.
They stay away
from storms.

They use radios. They find safe places to land.

Why Do We Need Them?

Pilots take us places. Off we go!

Pilot Facts

Tools

uniform

radio

controls

A Day in the Life

sit in the cockpit

use controls

land aircraft

Glossary

aircraft

machines that fly such as airplanes and helicopters

cockpits

the parts of aircraft where pilots sit

helicopters

aircraft that use spinning blades to fly

uniforms

clothes worn by pilots

To Learn More

ON THE WEB

FACTSURFER

Factsurfer.com gives you a safe, fun way to find more information.

1. Go to www.factsurfer.com.

2. Enter "pilots" into the search box and click 🔍.

3. Select your book cover to see a list of related content.

Index

aircraft, 12, 13
airplanes, 6
check, 12
cockpits, 6, 7
controls, 14, 15
fly, 4, 6, 8, 12, 16
hats, 10
helicopters, 6

land, 18
people, 8
radios, 18, 19
safe, 16, 18
steer, 14
storms, 16
take off, 14
ties, 10
uniforms, 10, 11

The images in this book are reproduced through the courtesy of: Luis Molinero, front cover, p. 23 (uniforms); art studio ideas, p. 3; Svitlana Hulko, pp. 4-5; Vladimir Endovitskiy, p. 6; YAKOBCHUK VIACHESLAV, pp. 6-7; Drazen_, pp. 8-9; skodonnell, p. 10; FG Trade, pp. 10-11; Mystockimages, pp. 12-13; wsfurlan, pp. 14-15; Skycolors, pp. 16-17; halbergman, pp. 18-19, 22 (sit in the cockpit); NIKS ADS, p. 20; VanderWolf-Images, pp. 20-21; AboutLife, p. 22 (uniform); Nadezda Murmakova, p. 22 (radio); Jinny Goodman/ Alamy, p. 22 (controls); Nuttapong punna, p. 22 (use controls); Natalia Bostan, p. 22 (land aircraft); aappp, p. 23 (aircraft); Dushlik, p. 23 (cockpits); FotoDax, p. 23 (helicopters).